Tread Lightly

A Life Insurance Guide
for the Affluent Client

Arthur —

Thank you
for visiting our
Farm.

I hope you enjoy the read!

Mike

Tread Lightly

A Life Insurance Guide
for the Affluent Client

Michael R. Smith

TFP Brokerage
2014

Copyright © 2014 by Michael R. Smith
All rights reserved. This book or any portion thereof may not be reproduced or used in any manner whatsoever without the express written permission of the publisher except for the use of brief quotations in a book review or scholarly journal.

First Printing: 2014
ISBN: 1496171675
ISBN 978-1496171672
Library of Congress Control Number: 2014904772
CreateSpace Independent Publishing Platform,
North Charleston, South Carolina

The Financial Partners Group LLC
11138 State Bridge Road #100
Johns Creek, GA 30022
www.TreadLightlyGuide.com

Ordering Information:
Special discounts are available on quantity purchases
by corporations, associations, educators, and others.
For details, contact the publisher at the above listed address.
US trade bookstores and wholesaler,
please contact TFP Brokerage.
Tel: (678) 338-4380; Fax: (678) 281-7605;
Email: Help@TFPBrokerage.com

DEDICATION

Tread Lightly is the culmination of many hard years of dedication to this industry. However, my first priority has always been my family. It is through their support and sacrifice that any of this is possible, and I'm proud to take the opportunity to thank you for enriching my life.

Nick and Kennedy

To say I am a proud father would be a massive understatement. You have always been there for me and provided the inspiration to overcome life's obstacles. I love you dearly and I'm so thankful for your love and support. I am very proud of you both for not only your accomplishments and hard work, but for the people you have become. Nick: You have grown into a great young man and I can't wait to see where your life takes you. Keep up your diligent work ethic and dedication; I know it will carry you to great success in whatever you attempt.

Kennedy: Thank you for your love and for providing me constant inspiration. I am amazed at the high standards you impose on yourself, all while maintaining great friendships and an extremely active social calendar. Watching you grow into the beautiful and accomplished young lady that you are today has been a true gift. Just as with your brother, the sky is your limit, and I can't wait to see where your potential takes you.

Dawn

Thank you for your positive spirit and the love you have delivered into my life. You have supported me tirelessly through this project while offering me encouragement to finish the task. Knowing you are in my corner gives me the confidence to take on any challenge, and I'm a very lucky man to be facing the world with you by my side.

To *my sister, brother-in-law, and their family, Kim, Bert, Tripp, and Wyatt Loflin:* You have provided me with love and support throughout my entire life, and I'm thankful for our relationship. *Lastly, to my parents, Charlie and Janet Smith:* Thank you for providing me with the love, motivation, and integrity that have allowed me to remain focused on getting projects done the right way for the right reasons. Without you both, none of this would be possible.

TABLE OF CONTENT

PREFACE

The idea behind this book didn't spark from an extraordinary series of events, but instead came out of the natural progression of our business practice.

Far too often in this industry, we see professional biases develop that are rarely in the best interest of the client. There are many factors that lead to the emergence of such biases, but they are almost always driven by compensation, carrier/agency rewards, employee benefits, and sales pressure. The effect is often an environment where personal rewards are weighted more heavily than advocating for the client's best interest.

Unfortunately, this is a major component of how the life insurance business works, and it is impossible to explain how to navigate the process of correctly obtaining insurance without addressing these issues. It is the reason why we use the phrase "tread lightly"; just by understanding that this kind of culture exists, you are already on the road ensuring that you will secure the right type of insurance for your needs that will still be in force at the time of your death. We will continue to call this *our definition of success*.

In short, there are real, tangible obstacles potentially blocking you from achieving your goal of getting the best deal and coverage possible. Because of this, we at TFP are constantly reviewing the policies we place and brainstorming new ideas about how we can grow as an advocacy-based firm. That is precisely how we created our Partnership Program, which quickly became a defining feature of our agency. One of the purposes of our Partnership Program is to form strategic relationships with client advocates. By doing this, we hope to ensure that client advocates have the proper support systems to confidently and competently provide their clients with quality life insurance guidance and information.

As we will address in this book, oftentimes the policyholder's life insurance is not performing in the way it was initially described. This creates a chain reaction where clients are making crucial decisions regarding both financial and estate planning without fully understanding their policy or how it works. This issue is an epidemic in the life insurance industry, but can be avoided with proper due diligence.

The process of writing this book began with these questions: *"How can we, in a neutral and nonthreatening way, provide consumers with the best information possible on how to maintain or purchase life insurance? How can we teach potential life insurance buyers how to protect themselves when making a sizable insurance investment?"*

Over the years, we had created numerous tools and guides for our clients' benefit, and as we examined these materials, we realized that we had developed an effective, no-nonsense set of tools to guide our clients through the entire process of obtaining life insurance.

What started as a collection of checklists has now grown into an effective overview of what must be accomplished in order to purchase, manage, and protect a sizable amount of insurance. As we continued to develop these ideas, we also saw a great need for a resource to guide *client advocates* such as attorneys, CPAs, trust officers, fiduciaries, and other professionals who represent both businesses and individual clients; we extend this term to any representative tasked with guiding their clients through the insurance-buying process, but who aren't experts in this industry.

We have encountered numerous high-functioning, efficient people who are tremendously intelligent, yet have had difficulty purchasing or managing their life insurance. As a result, we established internal guides for our advisors and clients to follow, and now feel that this book can help others in the same way.

We titled the book *Tread Lightly* because not only is it an office motto of sorts, but we want it to be clear from cover to cover: *be careful.* If you own a lot of insurance or plan on purchasing a sizable policy, you need to make sure that you understand the proper steps involved and can trust that your advisor is advocating for your best interests. *Mistakes in this arena cost millions!*

Personally, I'm excited that this book will serve as a new step in our continued commitment to advocate, educate, and partner with advisors and consumers alike. Our goal is simple: by strengthening the advocacy elements of the life insurance industry, we can better protect the financial future of all parties involved.

I hope you enjoy the read.

Mike Smith, CLU
President of TFP Brokerage, LLC

WHAT IS *TREAD LIGHTLY?*

"Tread lightly" is a colloquialism we at TFP often use around the office. For the uninitiated, it means that you should be careful about the decisions you make, as you can very easily cause yourself irrevocable damage.

Life insurance is a complex, confusing product, and mistakes regarding either an in-force policy or the purchase of a large amount of insurance can be dramatic and costly. If you are somehow involved in the management or purchase of large amounts of life insurance, this guide will give you clear directions on how to navigate that process.

WHAT THIS BOOK IS NOT

- An attempt to sell a product or carrier's portfolio
- A sales tool for anyone attempting to sell life insurance
- A presentation guide to help licensed insurance agents sell more insurance
- A reference guide for terms and definitions pertaining to life insurance
- An introduction for consumers looking to understand and purchase term and other less complicated forms of insurance
- A comprehensive guide to life insurance

WHO IS TFP BROKERAGE?

The Financial Partners Brokerage (TFP) is an independent life insurance brokerage general agency. We are equity members of AimcoR Group LLC, a national insurance marketing organization that represents the interests of thirty-eight independent brokerage general agencies across the United States. We also maintain a traditional broker dealer relationship with Financial Telesis Inc.

I founded TFP in 2008 as an extension of my general agency. Initially, our goal was to better promote other products and services to my agency advisory team. The roots of TFP date all the way back to 1983 when I first joined the life insurance industry. TFP is a Georgia LLC with four member owners. We became completely independent from any carrier in 2011.

Our initiatives are supported through the formation and maintenance of strategic partnerships with unique professional firms. Some of our partner-firms offer financial and insurance advice but are in need of specific expertise within the life insurance industry, while others are seasoned advisory practices looking for broad market product access, quality processing, and advanced guidance.

The processes and checklists we have developed over the years are the key to achieving our definition of success when it comes to owning or maintaining life insurance. You will find them in this book and on *TreadLightlyGuide.com*. To learn more about our Partnership Program, please visit *www.tfppartnership.com*.

OUR DEFINITION OF SUCCESS

When purchasing large amounts of insurance, there is no "one-size-fits-all" approach. There is no cookie-cutter solution to complicated insurance needs, and each individual will have a very specific set of goals that must be accomplished. Oftentimes, we will refer to our "definition of success", which references the broad set of goals that each client must achieve to properly own and maintain his or her insurance, because this industry's scary truth is simple: many permanent life insurance policies will not always pay off at the time of the insured's death.

Steps to Achieving Our Definition of Success

_____ **Obstacles**
_____ **Advisor**
_____ **Policy**
_____ **Underwriting**
_____ **Maintenance**

TREAD LIGHTLY'S
DEFINITION OF SUCCESS

*To purchase life insurance in the most cost-efficient manner possible, and to maintain that insurance effectively throughout the life of the contract. In order to be successful, life insurance consumers must be educated throughout the entire process so that they understand the ramifications of the decisions they are making. The ultimate goal for every policy owner should be that the desired policy **pays off at the insured's death.***

INTRODUCTION

Let's start with a little addition by subtraction. Because of both the size and specializations of this industry, we simply can't cover everything about insurance in this brief guide. If we set out to cover all the basics of this industry, this guide would turn into a 400-page reference manual about life insurance, and our message would quickly become diluted. Our goal is to get you the information you need to *achieve our definition of success*—the payoff of the in-force insurance policy at the time of the insured's death.

To be clear, this is not a book to learn more about term insurance, nor is it a high-level overview of all the moving parts in a life insurance policy.

READERS WHO WILL BENEFIT MOST FROM TREAD LIGHTLY

1. AFFLUENT CLIENTS WHO NEED TO PURCHASE LARGE AMOUNTS OF LIFE INSURANCE

2. AFFLUENT CLIENTS WHO OWN LARGE AMOUNTS OF LIFE INSURANCE

3. CLIENT ADVOCATES, OR ANYONE TASKED WITH REPRESENTING THE CLIENT; REGARDLESS OF WHETHER YOU ARE AN ACCOUNTANT, ATTORNEY, OR OTHER INDUSTRY PROFESSIONAL, YOUR ONE COMMON INTEREST WILL BE TO REPRESENT THE CONSUMER AND HELP YOUR CLIENT MANAGE AN EXISTING INSURANCE PORTFOLIO OR PURCHASE A LARGE AMOUNT OF LIFE INSURANCE IN THE APPROPRIATE WAY.

4. INSURANCE AGENTS AND FINANCIAL ADVISORS WHO ARE INVOLVED IN THE MAINTENANCE OR PURCHASE OF SUBSTANTIAL AMOUNTS OF LIFE INSURANCE

5. TRUSTEES OF IRREVOCABLE LIFE INSURANCE TRUSTS

6. TRUST DEPARTMENTS INVOLVED IN PURCHASING OR MANAGING LIFE INSURANCE POLICIES

7. EMPLOYEES OF FAMILY OFFICES

We won't delve into the mechanics of whole life insurance or cover all the messy details found in modern insurance policy illustrations. Likewise, our purpose is not to explain the specifics of the medical underwriting process or to outline the unique roles of all the cast members involved.

If this is your need, there are other more comprehensive, "voluminous" reference books available (our office recommends Tony Steuer's *Questions and Answers on Life Insurance: The Life Insurance Toolbook*). Unfortunately, a cumbersome introduction and explanation of the industry would be an impediment to our purpose.

At the end of the day, your goal should be to know the right questions to ask so you can make informed decisions about your portfolio. We are assuming that you have a relative understanding regarding your insurance needs and have a rudimentary comprehension of the basics of life insurance. Whether you are looking to secure a policy for yourself, or you are a client advocate representing a consumer, the main beneficiary of the material outlined herein will be any person charged with making or maintaining a sizable insurance purchase.

Tread Lightly will help you understand the questions you should be asking your advisor and the carrier. We believe these questions will help you avoid making costly errors while you are obtaining critical information regarding the purchase and maintenance of your portfolio.

Regardless of what you buy, *we believe that there is a right and wrong way to purchase insurance.* Even simple oversights can cause problems if the appropriate questions are not asked. We know there are many qualified advisors that understand this, but as we started developing this book, we were genuinely surprised at the lack quality conversations, in print or online, outlining an advisory approach to purchasing or maintaining a life insurance portfolio.

However niche a concept it proves, there is an inherent need for quality, consumer-focused dialogue about protecting the client's best interests throughout the complex process of large insurance purchases.

The unfortunate truth is that we are often called in to fix failing policies every day. There is the high likelihood that a percentage of our readers with permanent insurance have policies that are not performing anywhere close to their original projections. Our practice has been built from the ground up to help rectify costly errors like these. We intentionally make no mention of any carriers as we have no intention of attacking any particular business or creating a bias for or against any particular company or agent.

Our promise is that you'll find no sales pitch in this book. It's important to add that these aren't just scare tactics; after a lifetime in this industry, my associates and I have found a very clear pattern of where insurance goes wrong.

I've spent over twenty years as both a general agent and a branch manager for two large insurance companies. After years of enduring the status quo, I walked away to start The Financial Partners Group LLC because I believed that there could be a better, more client-focused approach for an insurance firm.

Thus, I went from running organizations with multiple offices in five different states, overseeing and managing tens of thousands of policyholders, to a small boutique firm that focused solely on the consumer's best interests.

As an agency manager, I directly oversaw many of the issues we will touch on in the first chapter. These experiences have given me a unique perspective on the marketplace and the clients who are most adversely affected by major life insurance blunders.

Outlined in this book is a system developed from years of partnerships with other like-minded professionals, created as a guide to help you understand the primary problems you will face in securing a policy, and the pertinent questions you must ask to ensure that you or your client advocate receives the appropriate information. We believe it is time to demand a higher standard for our industry, and so we must provide advisors with more effective tools to better serve their clients.

I'd also like to note that if you've picked up this book because you are interested in gearing your marketing toward a certain type of clientele, we have outlined a system of accountability that can help you in the same way it helps the client. Our goals are for you to be a better advisor and for the client to be a more educated buyer. Together we can work to move this industry away from its past and into a new age of transparency.

SECTION ONE:
OBSTACLES TO SUCCESS

This section outlines a broad overview of the major obstacles that stand as potential barriers to achieving our definition of success. If you fully understand these issues, you will be a more informed buyer, which is especially important in dealing with an industry that often benefits from uninformed consumers. By being unable to advocate for yourself, you can be susceptible to costly mistakes.

ELEVEN INDUSTRY OBSTACLES FOR THE UNINITIATED BUYER

There are many obstacles that you will face in obtaining and properly maintaining a life insurance portfolio. Some are tangible, concrete needs that require clear steps to ensure that your existing policy will be properly managed. Other issues are more abstract and concern the industry as a whole. The more informed you are, the more satisfactory your life insurance experiences will be. By just being aware that some of these issues exist, you are taking a giant step forward toward being a successful insurance owner.

Many of the obstacles you face could easily fill that hypothetical 400-page book we talked about earlier, and you may find that you would like a more in-depth explanation of certain obstacles. However, the purpose of this guide is to provide you the essential information you need as efficiently as possible. While we want to adequately cover the problems you will face, this book is not a comprehensive guide to the life insurance industry. Our objective isn't to try to teach you the business, just to provide you with the basic information we believe is absolutely necessary for anyone involved in a complicated life insurance transaction.

If you plan on purchasing a sizable life insurance policy or already have a portfolio in-force, you immediately have two major obstacles standing in your way: *compensation* and *distribution*.

I believe that the compensation structure in this industry is broken and in need of a major overhaul, as it is the direct cause of countless failed policies. Distribution doesn't necessarily have to be a problem for you, but you must be aware that these kinds of minefields exist. In response, we have dedicated an entire chapter to understanding how to find the right type of advisor to help navigate the insurance buying and ownership process.

Agents are trained and coached to sell, not advocate. This is largely due to "revolving door" employment that is part of the nature of this industry. However, this is also because insurance policies are very complicated, and it takes a high level of training to interpret today's illustrations and policies—a level of understanding few licensed agents possess.

Unfortunately, many people who play a role in owning or buying insurance don't know the right questions to ask or have a reliable process to follow to aid in managing or purchasing life insurance.

While we can't dive into all of this industry's problems, we can address the most prevalent issues and arm you with the right questions to ask—so let's get started.

Steps to Achieving Our Definition of Success

_____ **Obstacles**
_____ **Advisor**
_____ **Policy**
_____ **Underwriting**
_____ **Maintenance**

Industry Obstacles at a Glance

Life insurance is an often overlooked tool for maintaining an effective financial strategy. It is far more than a means to an end, and when used effectively should be an incredible agent for good. Unfortunately, a vast number of US citizens are underinsured, in part because many overestimate the cost of life insurance. However, when you have a multibillion-dollar industry that employs hundreds of thousands of salespeople, there will inevitably be problems.

In my experience, I have met hundreds of wonderful advisors who are a credit to this industry and the clients they serve. That said, I have also come across a rogue's gallery of unethical agents who hawk ineffective and expensive products to maintain their own extravagant lifestyles.

Agents like these are one of the reasons we have put this guide together. Finding a life insurance advisor you can trust is a crucial factor in getting an accurate survey of your financial outlook, and I sincerely believe that this book will help you find the right type of advisor to protect your own portfolio.

Of all the financial tools at your disposal, a life insurance portfolio is generally the least likely to be monitored and maintained. Because of our expertise, we see the aftermath of failed policies on a daily basis. While every situation is unique, one constant remains: it is far less time intensive and expensive to monitor a policy than to completely reinvent a client's portfolio.

Let me give you an example: we operate a referral-only advisory practice, and one of our clients recently took almost a $3 million loss on their previous insurance portfolio, *only to start all over again.* When major mistakes are made with large amounts of insurance, sometimes the only solution is to abandon the policies and completely rebuild the entire portfolio. It doesn't matter how much wealth you acquire over a lifetime; $3 million is a substantial amount of money to lose, especially when it could have been avoided. The fact that those policies had to be surrendered due to unnecessary errors is an egregious example of negligence. So why did this happen?

It turned out that these policies had been sold and then serviced improperly. By the time this family came to us for help, there weren't any palatable changes we could make to their existing portfolio that would match their objectives. They had to walk away from those policies and start the process all over again. Not only did they lose the money, but this was also a substantial time investment on behalf of their advisory team that could have otherwise been focused on other needs.

So what happened? An agent sold the family No-Lapse Universal Life policies that were all minimally funded in order to make them look attractive to the client; in short, they were set up as term policies but sold as permanent insurance. Only one of these policies were expected to last the insured's entire life expectancy. The family also had variable insurance with no diversification. One hundred percent of the cash value was allocated to S&P 500 Index funds. It is worth noting that over forty different types of investments were available to the client, but only one fund was selected.

The family clearly had the objective of having their insurance in-force at the death of the insured, regardless of how long this person ended up living. When we first started working with the family and their team, they were suspicious that their insurance may have not been working according to their expectations. However, they could not find a way to review each policy and compare the actual performance to their initial projections.

By the time this case came across my desk, there had already been two agents on the case who were unable to get the correct information for this family. The larger the policy, the more complicated sorting out related information becomes.

In this situation, the family had a great client advocate that worked tirelessly with our firm to secure the appropriate type and amount of insurance. We are confident both the family and their business will be protected for years to come. However, not every story has a happy ending, and the unfortunate fact is that many times these errors go unnoticed until the policy has imploded or lapsed. Not every client has the cash reserves and liquidity to completely start fresh—so *tread lightly*!

Soon you will have the knowledge to both purchase new insurance and manage existing contracts. Hopefully, our book will give you a better understanding of how to advocate for yourself and ensure that you have secured the right advisor who will work for your best interests.

Obstacle 1: Policy Reviews

If you already have insurance, the first step is to have your life insurance portfolio reviewed by a knowledgeable life insurance professional. If your policy hasn't been reviewed since the time it was purchased or within the past two years, you owe it to yourself to make sure it is appropriately performing to meet your objectives. You will later find tools in this book that will support you in your efforts to conduct an appropriate policy review.

As you advocate for yourself, be aware of how your policy is performing. Is it meeting your own objectives? If it is not, how do these policies need to be modified in order to ensure they are meeting your goals? Are there scenarios where a new policy would better fit your needs, or is your current portfolio maintaining its objectives? Until you know the answers to these questions, there is no way to be certain that you are properly protected.

To start, it is essential that you have a full understanding of your current objectives and goals; we recommend that you have a rudimentary understanding of your goals before you speak with an agent. A good advisor will be able to tell you if you have accurately assessed your situation. Put your needs in writing; don't worry about the numbers at first. It is important to be as clear as possible regarding your personal life insurance objectives. When you are sure of your goals, create a written policy statement, which you should ultimately keep with your policy.

Without a doubt, the most common and avoidable mistake is when a policy owner neglects to review his or her insurance portfolio. We recommend having your policy reviewed at least every two years, as this proactive approach can help you avoid being blindsided by a variety of issues (many of which are covered in part 2).

If you are the current owner of a life insurance portfolio, or a client advocate representing someone with a life insurance portfolio, those policies *must* be reviewed on regular basis. We cannot overstate the importance of this habit. Without reviewing existing policies, there is no way of knowing how a portfolio is performing and whether it is meeting the owner's needs.

Consider the following steps as you embark upon your review process:

Policy Review Steps

- State your objectives in writing and keep this policy statement with each contract.

- Get an in-force ledger at least every two years.

- Determine whether the portfolio is meeting your objectives.

- Visit *www.TreadLightlyGuide.com* to retrieve checklists by product and sample request letters.

- Ascertain that your in-force portfolio is meeting your objectives. If not, can the current portfolio be modified to meet your objectives?

- Evaluate options to see whether an alternative can better meet your needs.

If you have an advisor whom you trust who follows a process similar to the one outlined in chapter 2, you are already on the right track. If you are unsure whether this is the case or your advisor is unable to succinctly and appropriately outline his or her own process, we recommend using our system or finding another advisor that offers a clear and straightforward review process. Remember, you are never locked in to an advisor; you can always make an agent change.

It is also important to know that any reputable advisor will service your insurance, regardless of carrier. Changing advisors simply requires submitting an agent of record letter to that insurance carrier. When we find a carrier who won't allow an agent of record change, we simply provide the client with the proper documentation so that he or she can obtain policy review materials from the carrier directly. Either way, an advocacy-based advisor can help you get what is needed to conduct a professional policy review.

Throughout this process, it will become evident whether or not you are dealing with the type of advisor who can adequately service your insurance needs. Unfortunately, correctly performing a professional policy review is often beyond the capabilities of a high percentage of agents.

Obstacle 2: Agent Compensation

Disclaimer. There are many perfectly capable insurance agents in the field today. Some of them work with carriers while others are independent. It is not our goal to steer you in one direction or to advise you against a certain type of agent. We seek only to provide you with the necessary information to adequately assess whether an agent has the right capabilities to assist you in a large insurance transaction.

Make no mistake—while not having your policy reviewed is the biggest avoidable issue a consumer can face, the biggest threat to achieving our definition of success is the manner in which insurance agents are paid. At the risk of sounding redundant, agent compensation is the primary reason why a client must be vigilant in having the portfolio reviewed. In fact, agent compensation is arguably the top reason why certain policies collapse. Why is this?

An agent is typically paid forty to fifty times more commission in the first year of a written policy than in the years that follow. Furthermore, many carriers pay no agent compensation after the tenth year of the policy's life.

It doesn't take long to recognize that most carriers are paying agents to "sell" and not "service" your policies. This creates a scenario that is all too familiar within this industry: an agent sells a policy and then is rarely, if ever, in contact with the client again. This leaves clients to manage their own insurance portfolios with almost no education or training as to how these policies work. Is it any wonder why so many policyholders end up owning portfolios that they don't understand and that are not performing to their level of expectation?

Whether you believe this to be by design or simply an unfortunate evolution within the industry, large insurance carriers often benefit when policies do not live up to clients' expectations.

Carriers will profit from collecting premiums and not paying claims. Unfortunately, this is the current state of our industry, and it doesn't appear it will change any time soon. However, by educating yourself and following processes similar to those outlined in this book, we believe you will substantially reduce the risk of agent compensation being an obstacle to finding the best possible insurance solution.

Obstacle 3: Carriers

While there may be a wide range of issues that any given agent or client may have with life insurance carriers, these companies don't force anyone to purchase their policies. Ultimately, we choose a carrier and a product with the hope and expectation of what that policy should accomplish. However, this doesn't mean that the information provided to the client regarding a policy's performance will be clear—or even straightforward.

The biggest struggle I've had with carriers over the years is not receiving clear information to direct questions. As a client advocate, I know that trying to get accurate in-force ledgers can be a laborious process and can at times take months to get the correct information.

In terms of the "client experience," most carriers excel at filling their annual statements and summaries with information that is indecipherable to most consumers (and the majority of agents). Even when you know what specific information you need, carriers rarely provide that data in the format that is initially requested. It will likely take several requests to get exactly what is needed to conduct an appropriate policy review. We often find that carrier policyholder service representatives don't know the answers to many of the questions on our checklists.

Trying to obtain the right information is a struggle for even the most advanced advisors. Unless you are well trained, it is highly improbable you'll be able to understand what is provided in most carrier correspondence.

Thus, we highly recommend finding a life insurance professional who can guide you effectively through this process. Acumen and experience are the only ways to understand "carrier language," and this is gained only through years of industry exposure. As you begin to examine what type of agent would fit your needs best, *tread lightly*. Finding the right advisor is a critical step in achieving our definition of success.

Obstacle 4: Carrier-Affiliated Agents

There are two types of advisors you will come in contact with: independent and carrier-affiliated. While both types *may* have the skills necessary to help you achieve our definition of success, the two are very different and often do not yield similar results.

As you probably deduced, a carrier-affiliated agent is a semi-independent licensed life insurance agent who is aligned with a specific insurance carrier. Most full-time life insurance agents are carrier-affiliated.

Many of these agents are considered "statutory employees," which has a rare and unique definition under the IRS code. These agents are essentially independent contractors that are provided with employee benefits from their affiliated carrier.

There is significant potential for bias in these agents' carrier selection processes, as their ongoing retirement, employee benefits, and reward programs depend on their meeting a preset production quota of that specific carrier's products. Because of this, carriers have adeptly designed their compensation packages to entice affiliated agents to write more of their policies.

Agents are taught—and I have experienced this firsthand—that if agents understand their contract (specifically, what decisions will produce the most income and how agents can maintain their benefits), they will understand how to maximize their compensation and employee benefit plan. Generally speaking, the more business agents give their carrier, the higher their payout on each policy sold. Almost every incentive written into the agents' contracts are designed to sell more of that specific carrier's offerings. The result is the potential for overwhelming personal bias on the agent's account, regardless of the client's best interest.

This isn't necessarily harmful for every individual purchasing a life insurance policy, but as we said earlier, this book isn't for everyone. If you are a young, healthy person, buying a small term policy with a carrier-affiliated agent might cost a few dollars more per month than going with a competitor's similar, but less expensive plan. However, the repercussions change exponentially if you are buying a sizable amount of insurance.

If your agent of choice has a carrier bias, there is a legitimate possibility that your purchasing options could be limited to one carrier. In that situation, the prospective agent has ruled out your entire competitive market. This can be particularly crushing to middle-aged and older clients due to the fact that each carrier has different specialties regarding different conditions. In section 2, you'll find both a worksheet designed to help you understand your risk rating and the material you'll need to compare carrier offers. In case you are unaware, a "risk rating" is a predetermined risk-class an underwriter will assign to an applicant when that individual applies for a life insurance policy. An individual's lifestyle, family history, gender, and medical history all factor into this decision.

In working with carrier-affiliated agents (or any agent, for that matter), you must look at competing policies from various carriers. If not, you lose your leverage as a customer. Require that your agent provide you a spreadsheet of different plans, carriers, pricing, competitive underwriting analysis, and policy features (an example is shown on page 42).

Tread lightly; carrier-affiliated agents may trade under a business name that is different than the carrier's. This is called a DBA ("doing business as") and is very common. The carrier's compliance department will require a disclaimer on the agent's business card, website, and marketing materials that the insurance carrier is independent of the agent's DBA firm.

Review both sides of any advisor's business card to determine exactly with whom he or she is affiliated. If an insurance carrier's name is on that card, this means the agent is a carrier-affiliated agent.

Obstacle 5: New Agent Training

In most carrier-affiliated agencies you'll find some variation of an "activity management system" (e.g., one-card system). In the most simplistic terms, this is an activity scorecard method for new agents and is a ratio-based system to boost sales. The philosophy behind this system is to "work the numbers." It's ingenious, and it works.

However, clients quickly become a name in a card box and are processed through the activity system. The carrier-affiliated agent is taught that making a certain number of calls will lead to a percentage of scheduled appointments. It is proven that a percentage of these appointments lead to a benefits presentation. A smaller percentage of the presentations will lead to an opportunity to close business. At the end of the sales cycle, you have x number of policies on the books.

When entering the life insurance business, the standard protocol is for a potential agent to receive two weeks of sales training, which essentially amounts to a comprehensive explanation of the agency's activity management system. From my personal experience, there is very little training on the technical aspects of how policies are constructed or how to professionally advise clients. Agencies are not spending enough time teaching new agents how different policies work and what happens when "real-world" results do not match the policy's estimations. Ideally, new agents would have more in-depth training on how to provide legitimate advice and how projections change over time. However, these are sales-minded organizations with a vested interest in selling more products and therefore are not wholly motivated to take the time to educate new hires to advocate and support.

After their initial crash course in "effective selling," the new agent is then released to sell directly to the consumer. If they've taken their training to heart, they'll work hard to make as many calls as possible. In turn, a percentage of those calls will become appointments and will eventually lead to sales. My biggest concern is that these new agents typically call themselves *financial advisors*. Their elevator speech generally includes something along the lines of, "I help people build and protect their wealth."

I don't believe that the acclimation process allows these agents to be in a position to advise anyone on how to "build and protect wealth." To give an example, one of the major carriers we are referencing hired 5,000 new agents in 2012 and published a goal of 5,500 agents in 2013. It's a numbers game, just like the one-card system, and the more agents they hire, the more products they can sell.

We aren't saying that these agents aren't qualified to help you; most importantly, we aren't saying that they *can't* help you. However, you can ensure your own success by requiring that your agent take certain steps to guarantee that your insurance is purchased and managed properly, with you as an educated consumer.

The truth of the matter is that the average US citizen is grossly underinsured or completely uninsured. Both this system and these agents have great potential to solve the problem of the substantial lack of life insurance ownership in America. However, very little about this system works in the best interests of affluent clients.

This is potentially disastrous for individuals with a high net worth or client advocates in need of guidance on complex policy matters. An affluent client's portfolio must to be viewed as something more than a commission-based transaction, so tread lightly! We recommend that you follow a process similar to the one described in chapter 2 to find the advisor you need to guide you through the policy ownership process.

Obstacle 6: Persistency Bonuses

Most carrier-affiliated agent contracts contain a provision called a "persistency bonus." It is designed to compensate the agent for keeping in-force business on the books. This means that the more business agents keep in-force, the more they get paid.

Our primary concern with this provision is that a carrier-affiliated agent who is not advocacy-based is not likely to recommend a replacement of an in-force policy, even if it is in the best interest of the client. As a result, this could end up costing the policy owner a substantial amount of money. What most consumers do not understand is that replacing an in-force policy can have a substantial effect on a carrier-affiliated agent's renewal income. This is why you might find certain agents opposed to replacing an in-force policy, as it ultimately ends up costing them money.

What does that mean for the buyer? Even if your carrier-affiliated agent has better plans available, their system is constructed to discourage the agent from proactively advising their clients. Even if they are conducting periodic policy reviews, it is not in the best interest of carrier-affiliated agents to follow a process similar to ours; we recommend that the advisor always consider alternatives to a current portfolio if it makes more sense for the client.

As you may have guessed, the bigger the policy, the more it figures into persistency bonus compensation. Remember, replacement isn't always in the best interest of the client, but to the carrier-affiliated agent, replacing an in-force policy is a threat to renewal income. If a better policy is available, you may be less likely to hear about it with this particular type of agent.

Obstacle 7: Internal Replacement Rules for Carrier-Affiliated Agents

Most carrier-affiliated agent contracts contain internal replacement rules. These rules will either:

- Restrict the percentage of policy placements that are internal replacements, or

- Reduce or eliminate commissions on internal policy replacements.

Why is this important? Combined with the persistency bonus, this creates an environment that makes it very difficult for carrier-affiliated agents to follow a policy review process similar to the one we recommend. He or she has to actually stop short of the final step, which is to evaluate whether an alternative would be a better fit for the client. Under these rules, an agent can actually lose money by recommending a replacement for an in-force policy.

We are not saying that replacing an in-force policy always makes sense. Regardless of what rules an advisor has to follow, the replacement of a policy can create additional costs that might not be in your best interest. We believe that the policy review process should always include an analysis of whether an alternative to the in-force policy is a reasonable step in the ongoing evaluation of your policy. Look for an advisor that has no restrictions or penalties for showing you all of your options.

Obstacle 8: Carrier Bias

When it is time to apply for a policy, far too many agents are biased toward a particular carrier and consequently fail to follow an advisory-based evaluation process.

If you submit to a carrier before a life insurance professional has fully evaluated you as a risk, the process immediately shifts to favor the carrier. Good advisors will not leave your rating up to chance or circumstance. Remember, each carrier has different "sweet spots" pertaining to underwriting, and these niches are not limited to health conditions. Driving records, financial status, and lifestyle are all examples of how different carriers will evaluate risk. All of these elements can affect your rating with any carrier.

A carrier bias is most dangerous to your financial future in the situations where an agent recommends that a client submit an application for a life insurance policy without seeing what competing carriers are offering. To protect yourself, do your due diligence. We recommend never submitting an application for life insurance until you see a side-by-side analysis of comparable policies.

You are much more likely to get a better policy and a more favorable price if you follow processes similar to those outlined in this book.

Obstacle 9: General Agents, Sales Managers, and Agency Quotas

Each carrier-affiliated agency has a general agent (or GA) who oversees the agency and individual agents. The GA is directly responsible for answering to their carrier and meeting that carrier's set quotas.

In the event that a large amount of business in a carrier-affiliated organization is conducted outside "the family," it is the GA's job to exert his influence over the agent to place business with their carrier. A GA must be effective at doing this to maintain his or her job. There is a chain of command, and below the GA is the sales manager who has a similar set of goals, but on a smaller scale.

Within the world of the agent, general agents are very powerful. They exert great influence over the agent's proceedings, as they are responsible for the agent's relationship with the agency. This affects the agent's cost structure, sales leads, payout on business, incentive programs, and staff support. These are all particularly important details considering that these agents are "outside" contractors relying on that specific carrier's support and employee benefits.

This is not an attempt to condemn general agents or carrier-affiliated agencies. However, we find that most consumers are not aware of how these systems work. Remember, none of these aforementioned conflicts of interests are an issue if your advisor is showing you options via a multicarrier approach and following a process that requires negotiating with carriers prior to submitting a formal application. However, if the agent's immediate response to securing more insurance is to turn to their carrier, *tread lightly*.

Obstacle 10: Irrevocable Trust Notice Procedures

Most affluent people buy life insurance within a vehicle called an Irrevocable Life Insurance Trust (ILIT). The proper process to follow in overseeing an ILIT can be found in chapter 5 under the section Irrevocable Life Insurance Trust Checklist.

Many of the common mistakes we see with ILITs pertain to the annual gift tax exclusion. We rarely find that the annual notice procedures have been followed correctly. If those procedures are not followed, the annual gifts can be disallowed, causing those gifts to be included in the decedent's estate.

The frequency of this error makes it an easy target for an IRS agent in an estate audit. The unnecessary taxes caused by this mistake are often substantial and represent a terribly unjust cost due to a simple oversight. When considering the members of your ILIT advisory team, be sure it is clear who will be responsible for the annual notice compliance process.

Obstacle 11: Manipulating Sales Illustrations

Illustrations are a sales tool used to predict and project the future performance of a policy. In short, an illustration shows the factors of a policy and projects values and benefits over the remainder of your life. Illustrations are presented to give you an idea of how a policy will perform. Keep in mind that the data is all based on assumptions, and you need to be confident that the person running the illustration is using projections that are realistic.

When you think about it, illustrations simply cannot project performance as fact. Modern policies are too complex and have a multitude of advanced moving parts. In your own experience, what can you project out over the course of your life expectancy? It is unrealistic to assume that numbers being projected over the course of your lifetime will be accurate. These illustrations are no exception.

Many consumers do not fully understand that illustrations projecting the future are well-informed conjectures. Because of this, you must to be sure your advisor is using conservative, realistic assumptions; otherwise, the data within an illustration will be useless and misleading.

The main area of illustration abuse is policy-crediting rates, which can be adjusted within the illustration software. It is important to know at *what* rate the policy is being projected in the illustration, and most importantly, *why*. You should always know the rationale behind the crediting rate proposed.

Just as an example, every version of variable life illustration software I have seen will allow you to illustrate at a 12 percent annual return (or more). For this to hold true, you would have to receive a 12 percent return annually within the invested subaccounts. If you are buying a large policy and you live to life expectancy, you are likely to invest millions of dollars in this contract. Do you really want the success of your policy based on a 12 percent annual rate of return? We at TFP are not always comfortable using an 8 percent crediting rate on variable policies invested in the market, and we often recommend alternative projections at 6 percent.

I'd wager that if you asked any financial services professional to predict a percentage rate of return based on the stock market carried over a period of time equal to your life expectancy, he or she would tell you that this would be impossible. But if the advisor *had* to guess, I assure you it would be a conservative estimate and not 12 percent.

When you review an illustration, it is important to ask the advisor to explain all of the moving parts of the policy. Our policy purchase checklists in chapter 3 were created to help you ask the right questions throughout the process of buying policies.

When you do decide on a policy, you will have to sign a sales illustration indicating that you understand your purchase. Some illustrations are as long as eighty pages, and a signature is required to issue a policy. Even the most polished professionals will need a reference guide for some of the language and statements in these illustrations; state regulations and legal teams combine to make these already complex documents even harder for the client to understand. However, the insurance company will hold you accountable to whatever you sign, so *tread lightly.*

What is most important is that you understand the rationale behind the rates that these projections are based upon. You need to be provided data and an explanation to support the projections used.

In short, you need to be sure the assumptions used to project policy performance can be substantiated and are realistic.

Whether you have an existing policy or you are looking to purchase a new one, I believe the issues listed in these chapters could potentially impede you from obtaining the best deal possible on your insurance needs. There are many other problems that one faces when doing business with the life insurance industry, and we have (very broadly) covered the issues that could most directly affect you and keep you from achieving our definition of success. If you are somehow involved in a large insurance maintenance or purchase capacity, you now understand some of the obstacles you face.

Now that you know where the roadblocks are, it's time to find an advisor you can trust to secure the best policies to meet your needs.

Steps to Achieving
Our Definition of Success

__X__ Obstacles
_____ Advisor
_____ Policy
_____ Underwriting
_____ Maintenance

SECTION TWO:

THE FOUR STEPS OF SECURING AND MAINTAINING YOUR INSURANCE

In this section, you will find the advice, guides, and worksheets necessary to ensure that you are taking the appropriate steps to both purchase and maintain your insurance.

CHAPTER 2
STEP ONE:
FIND SOMEONE YOU TRUST

There are hundreds of thousands of active life insurance agents selling carrier products across the United States. A consumer in his or her midtwenties who is interested in purchasing a term policy will need an agent with a far less intensive level of sophistication than an affluent client with more complicated needs and preexisting health conditions.

When looking for agents, don't be afraid to consider their level of education and experience. Ask what type of insurance they generally write. We don't recommend a minimum level of experience in the industry, but you need to make sure your agent has a vast amount of experience purchasing the type of insurance you need.

When researching advisors, go to your state's insurance website and perform a search on your prospective agent. How many carriers is the advisor licensed with? If an advisor is not licensed with at least ten carriers, he or she is likely to be carrier-biased.

You can also access FINRA (Financial Industry Regulatory Authority, *finra.org*) to perform a search of the advisor's name, CRD, or location. FINRA logs all customer complaints, financial disclosures, outside business activities, and licenses held by the agent. However, just because there has been a financial complaint or disclosure doesn't mean an agent is incapable or dishonest.

If you find an advisor you like but there has been a complaint about him or her, ask your advisor about the instance directly. Oftentimes there are two sides to every story, and sometimes situations have extenuating circumstances. Agents are financial consultants and service providers, and getting information about how they operate (and how other clients have perceived they operate) can help empower you to make a well-educated decision.

Don't be afraid to use social media to your advantage. Most agents will have a LinkedIn account and list their areas of expertise; remember, you need a specialist, not someone who does "a little bit of everything." How an agent presents his LinkedIn account can be a great tool for gathering insight as to that advisor's areas of expertise and specializations.

Whomever you choose, make sure you are dealing with an insurance professional who deals with your type of needs on a regular basis.

To achieve our definition of success, make sure your advisor:

- Has a clear, written process for shopping the market and placing the insurance
- Presents you with multiple options from several different carriers (similar to the due diligence analysis on page 38)
- Works with an in-house underwriter or medical director who will negotiate with carriers on your behalf
- Commits to providing you a review of your insurance at least every two years while following a credible review process

If You Are Looking to Buy Insurance
We can't tell you which agent is right for you, but we can recommend that you take the time to find out about his or her

firm. What types of insurance do they specialize in? How many carriers are they licensed with? Do they operate in terms of volume, or are they more of a service-oriented agency? Does the firm have an outlined process similar to the ones contained in this book? How will the firm in question continue to service your policy over the years so that you are confident you will be provided with the advice and attention you need?

Review their marketing materials and ask about their lead processes. Find out to whom your advisor is marketing and who their clients are. Does the firm have a website or domain presence? Does the agency have a carrier-affiliated website or an independent website that describes its unique message and values? Do you agree with that site's content? What sort of business continuation plan does the firm have in place for when your advisor retires or passes on?

Finding the right agent is about finding the right fit for your needs. As we have discussed, there are generally two options available (carrier-affiliated and independent), and there are pros and cons to both.

Carrier-affiliated agencies will always have someone readily available to answer your questions, both present and future. Whenever you call, an agent should be available to pick up the phone and take your call. This is a major positive.

The downside is that you have no idea or control over who that agent will be. When selecting an agency without a clear continuation plan, you could be assigned to a new, unknown agent once your original agent is no longer practicing. It is very likely that this new agent will not receive compensation for servicing your policy. In a sales-based organization, the newly assigned carrier-affiliated agent is given little or no incentive to watch over your policy and provide you service.

There are also pros and cons with independent agents (anyone who isn't directly affiliated with a carrier and has a life insurance license). Independent agents could be banks, CPAs, or other entities where life insurance is not the primary business. Independent agents can also be investment advisors, financial advisors, or, like us, independent life insurance specialists.

One positive to choosing independent agents is that they most likely represent multiple carriers. However, be warned—you still must do your due diligence to make sure there isn't a carrier bias or some external influence pressuring the independent agent to write business with one carrier. Even if he or she is an independent advisor, volume growth leads to higher compensation. This means that the more business an agent places, the higher a payout could be with that specific carrier.

Another pro to dealing with independent agents is that it is very unlikely that their employee benefit program is incentivized by production with any specific carrier. Keep in mind that there can be incentive programs behind carrier relationships, such as bonuses, trips, and prizes, but this should never be a factor in how a client is advised in insurance matters.

The downside to working with independent agents is the threat of having no business continuation plan. What happens to the service of your policy if the agent is rendered disabled, dies, or retires? This can put you in an unfavorable position as the client advocate or the policy owner because you are left to deal directly with the carrier. By now, you can understand how difficult and frustrating that can prove to be.

So is there a right solution? We believe that both carrier-affiliated agents and independent agents are viable options, so long as they follow the right processes and have a written business continuation plan to ensure you have consistent service and advice for the rest of your policy's life.

Understanding Your Advisor and the Firm

As I've stated several times, the best services this industry can provide its clients are advocacy and proper due diligence. I've seen too many former associates take shortcuts in the advisory process due to both poor training and sales pressure.

Perhaps the most common shortcut I've noticed is agents not taking the appropriate steps to ensure that their clients are properly informed as insurance buyers and owners. This process should require not only the completion of the client's full medical file and relevant information, but also a consultation with the firm's staff medical director or underwriter. This must take place prior to any items being submitted to the carrier.

A great clue for determining if an advisor has the proper application process in place is to determine whether he or she uses a proprietary HIPAA (Health Insurance Portability and Accountability Act) form or a HIPAA form from a specific carrier. It is an agent's responsibility to use the correct software and websites to contact a reasonable number of potential carriers and gather their informal responses on risk-class ratings. The advisor should then summarize the collected responses and provide the client with legitimate options. Only at this time can a client fully contemplate the available options and make an educated decision. By this point, it is generally obvious which carrier is the logical choice.

Due Diligence Guide

Your needs are unique to your particular situation, and anyone who believes that there is a one-size-fits-all solution for your insurance probably does not understand the complexities of this business. When you are buying a modest amount of term insurance, the differences in policies will be minimal. However, when your insurance needs are in the millions, the difference in premiums and benefits can be millions of dollars. *Tread lightly!*

The due diligence example showcased in this section was prepared for an actual client. The table below represents an informal estimate for insurance that was actually placed. In our due diligence period, we gathered the records and pertinent details before reaching out to carriers informally to find out:

- What table rating the individual carriers evaluated our client at, and
- An estimate of the client's premium when taking into account his or her insurance needs and table rating *(remember: each carrier has its own specialties in regards to various conditions).*

Because of this client's medical issues, he was rated poorly by all but one carrier that happened to specialize in the client's condition. Carrier one's estimated premium was $162,200 less annually than the highest carrier estimate. This is a very clear example of why it is imperative to see your insurability shopped to as many carriers as possible; the differences in premium estimates are often substantial.

Due Diligence Analysis

Carrier	Risk-Class Ratings	Premium Estimate
Carrier 1	B	$118,750
Carrier 2	Postpone	Postpone
Carrier 3	F	$192,375
Carrier 4	D	$152,600
Carrier 5	F	$200,690
Carrier 6	D	$175,800
Carrier 7	F	$224,500
Carrier 8	F	$185,000
Carrier 9	F	$155,850
Carrier 10	H	$280,950
Carrier 11	H	$240,300
Carrier 12	F	$197,400

This is an example comparing ten-year term rates and policies. This analysis becomes even more complicated when comparing permanent insurance plans. Ask your advisor for an example of his or her due diligence analysis to ensure you are selecting the right firm.

Business Continuation

When evaluating an advisory firm, there are many elements to consider beyond your understanding of its advisory process. Before you begin, how long do you hope to own a policy portfolio before you die? Once you know this, determine if your firm or advisor of choice will still be in the industry at the end of your life expectancy. It is important to consider who will service your policy if your advisor is no longer managing insurance.

You are obviously not going to want to make a complex and large insurance purchase through an advisor with little-to-no experience. While I am not suggesting that this person will be technically incapable of an admirable performance, most clients in similar positions prefer experience to youth.

If your chosen advisor has considerable industry experience, you want to be sure that his or her agency has a solid continuation plan in place. In most cases, an agent with enough experience to appropriately handle complex policy placements is similar in age to the client who has accumulated a sizable amount of wealth.

Business continuation issues may arise ten, twenty-five, or fifty years after the purchase of a policy. The best agencies have a well-organized, written continuation plan for their firms. Look for continuation plans that have a multigenerational approach to mentoring new advisors so that you can expect a similar level of advocacy from the person who replaces your advisor. When I was the general agent for a carrier-affiliated agency, if an advisor moved on (retired, passed away, or just left the firm), it was up to my management team to decide who managed that book of business.

You don't want to find yourself in a situation where you are no longer in control of who is managing your insurance. Find an organization that is multigenerational with a consistent philosophical message and approach to your business. You will likely live well past your selected agent's tenure in this business, so *tread lightly*.

Don't End Up an Orphan

In this business, an "orphan" is an in-force policy that does not have an agent assigned to service it. You must be vigilant to ensure that your policy is never orphaned. Unfortunately, a majority of life insurance policies will end up orphaned and without the proper guidance to ensure that they are maintained effectively.

In the carrier-affiliated world, orphaned policies typically go to new agents, generally with little thought process. Most of the time there is no compensation paid to the new agent on an orphan policy, so his or her only incentive to speak with you is to sell you something new. Even worse, your private information has gone into the hands of a stranger you had no input in selecting.

Life Insurance Advisor Selection Process Checklist

Agent/firm name:
Carrier-affiliated agent? If so, which carrier?
Independent advisor?
Licensed with multiple carriers? How many?
Website? Is it carrier-affiliated or independent?
LinkedIn profile? Does profile exemplify an ability to meet your needs?
FINRA check? Any area(s) of concern?
Do they specialize in working in your area of need?
Multicarrier HIPAA (Health Insurance Portability and Accountability Act)?
Have you been provided an example of their multicarrier policy comparison?
Have you determined their in-force policy review process?
Do they have a written business continuation plan in place?
Have you met your advisor's successor? Is the plan multigenerational?

This checklist combines many of the criteria we have established as desirable attributes in a life insurance advisor. Use this when determining whether a prospective advisor is right for your needs.

The Bottom Line

Steps to Achieving Our Definition of Success
X __ **Obstacles**
X __ **Advisor**
____ **Policy**
____ **Underwriting**
____ **Maintenance**

Educated advisors and educated clients should never be mutually exclusive concepts. No advisor should be threatened by your knowledge of products or your desire to understand an illustration placed in front of you. Still, you are not supposed to be an expert on life insurance, and every professional knows this, so they should be willing to explain at length whatever you need to understand to be an educated buyer.

The reason we outline this information is to benefit both parties regarding the placement of insurance. Our industry needs a higher standard that rewards the advisor who puts a greater emphasis on client maintenance rather than just the sale.

Find someone that you trust who will commit to following the proper processes while making sure there is a business continuation plan in place. Remember, the questions that aren't asked are the ones that end up hurting you the most.

CHAPTER 3

STEP TWO:
SELECTING A POLICY

Now that you have a high-level understanding of some of the obstacles you may face and have selected your advisor, it's time to choose the proper policy or policies to fit your needs. We believe it is more than possible for you to ethically and effectively secure the right kind of insurance, especially if you know the right questions to ask.

You may have noticed that there is no glossary in this book. As we explained earlier, it is not our intent to offer an in-depth overview of the life insurance industry, but to help you navigate the pitfalls of policy purchase and maintenance. We simply cannot include every term, definition, and process description, or our core message would be lost.

This chapter's worksheets will help you outline the questions you need answered by your advisor when purchasing a policy. If your advisor has an understanding of your insurance needs and the information you will require before taking delivery of a policy, we believe you will have a more thorough understanding of the insurance you own.

There may be terms mentioned in the following sections that you have not heard of. It is our hope that the lack of definitions will prompt more meaningful discussions with your respective advisors; your insurance agent or client advocate will be able to appropriately explain to you the context or purpose of any unknown terms.

If you have particular questions, *www.TreadLightlyGuide.com* will continue to serve as a resource for additional inquiries.

The Checklists

As you know, our goal is to ensure that you are buying your insurance in a responsible, prudent way that will keep you from becoming a disgruntled policy owner. You simply can't know what you don't know, which is why we use these checklists in our business and have decided to share them in this book. Our intent is for these checklists to take you down a path in partnership with whoever is advising you on your policy decisions so that you are getting the proper information while making these critical decisions.

It is entirely possible that even the most competent advisors will not be able to immediately answer all the questions on any given worksheet. Off the top of my head, I wouldn't be able to answer many of the questions outlined below, especially those regarding the different carriers and products we offer. However, I know that as an advisor my job is to read the illustrations and do my research to be absolutely sure I am performing the proper due diligence for my clients. In the end, your advisor needs to find you the answers to the questions on these checklists so that you can make informed decisions.

Life Insurance Rating Services

There are several highly reputable insurance-rating services in the marketplace. These services exist to give policyholders and advisors a means of examining third-party ratings and an analysis of the individual investment strength, financial stability, and assessed risk of any given insurance organization.

The three rating services we use on these checklists are AM Best, Comdex, and Alirt. These are established companies well known to investors worldwide. I would recommend that you perform your own search as well, but these can help you make better, more informed decisions with any potential carrier. A more thorough study on how to assess carrier financial strength is included in the book's appendix.

Term Life Policy Purchase Checklist

Term insurance is a fairly simple product. It builds no cash value and typically has a guaranteed fixed premium for a limited period of time.

The biggest mistake we see consumers make when buying term insurance is that they don't know if they have purchased a true term policy or a term/universal life policy. The difference is that the term/universal life policy does not have a traditional conversion option. If you want to continue that policy past the guaranteed period of time, you must understand the set policy details (as opposed to buying an actual convertible policy and converting it into some form of a permanent plan).

The answers to the questions on this checklist will help you determine whether a term policy will meet your needs.

CARRIER / POLICY NAME:
Carrier Rating AM Best:
Carrier Rating Comdex:
Carrier Rating ALIRT:
Is the carrier on any rating company's watch list?
Is there any public information on the carrier that could affect future ratings?

Is the recommended policy
true term or a term/UL policy?

Is there a premium guarantee?
How long does it last?

Is the policy convertible?
For how long?

Can the policy face amount
be reduced post-issue?

What products are available
for conversion purposes?

What are the riders illustrated?

Did you follow the Life Insurance
Underwriting Process Guideline Checklist?

Have you been provided with a
financial profile on the carrier
(such as ALIRT or VitalSigns)?

Were you provided a final illustration that
exactly matches the policy that was issued?

Have you verified that ownership
and beneficiary designations are correct?

Has your agent committed to
providing an in-force ledger at
least every two years?

Are there carrier incentives
tied to the sale of this policy?

Whole Life Policy Purchase Checklist

Whole life insurance is a complicated, expensive, and extremely opaque product. The performance of whole life insurance almost always depends on the dividends, though dividends are far more volatile than most understand.

The primary mistakes most policyholders make revolve around crediting rates and understanding how participating dividends work. If you are looking at buying a policy that uses participating dividends, then you need to be confident that those dividends will perform for you; otherwise, you will not get a reasonable return on your investment and will be paying too much for that coverage.

Before purchasing one of these policies, it is important to get a written explanation regarding the carrier's dividend-crediting strategy. With this, you can better understand the effects of the changing interest rate environment and crediting rate on the performance of your policy.

This is the most common form of permanent insurance sold in the marketplace, but the majority of people selling these products will not be able to answer all of the questions on the checklist. That doesn't mean that you shouldn't be receptive to this type of policy if you believe it meets your needs, and it certainly doesn't mean that an advisor is misleading you or being dishonest if he or she can't initially answer these questions. Eventually, your advisor will need to supply you with this information and also be able to answer these questions in their proper context.

The answers to the questions on this checklist will help you determine whether a whole life policy will perform as projected and whether it will meet your needs.

CARRIER / POLICY NAME:

Carrier Rating AM Best:

Carrier Rating Comdex:

Carrier Rating ALIRT:

Is the carrier on any
rating company's watch list?

Is there any public information on the
carrier that could affect future ratings?

Are the nonforfeiture values'
crediting rates illustrated?

What is the illustrated
dividend-crediting rate?

How are dividend-crediting
rates determined?

Have you received a written
explanation from the carrier as to
how the dividends are determined?

What is the current general
account return of the carrier?

What dividend option has
been illustrated?

What riders are illustrated?

What is the loan rate of
policy? Is it variable or fixed?

How is the loan rate determined?

Do loans against the policy
affect future dividends?

Did you follow the Life Insurance
Underwriting Process Guideline Checklist?

Have you been provided with a
financial profile on the carrier
(such as ALIRT or VitalSigns)?

Were you provided a final
illustration that *exactly* matches
the policy that was issued?

Have you verified that ownership
and beneficiary designations are correct?

Has your agent committed to
providing you an in-force ledger
at least every two years?

Are there carrier incentives tied
to the sale of this policy?

Universal Life Policy Purchase Checklist

Universal life is a complicated product that contains interest, expense, and mortality risk.

The most common mistake we see with universal life pertains to interest rate fluctuations. The policy is often sold at a crediting rate that is higher than the carrier returns during the life of the contract. The policyholder ends up owning a policy that will lapse well before his or her death due to the contract being underfunded. This happens frequently, so make sure you clearly understand the assumptions your policy projections are based upon and the rationale behind projecting policy values at that rate.

The answers to the questions on this checklist will help you determine whether a universal life policy will perform as projected and whether it will meet your needs.

CARRIER / POLICY NAME:

Carrier Rating AM Best:

Carrier Rating Comdex:

Carrier Rating ALIRT:

Is the carrier on any rating company's watch list?

Is there any public information on the carrier that could affect future ratings?

What is the crediting rate illustrated?

Is there a minimum interest rate guarantee?

Did you receive an illustration at 1 percent below current crediting rate?

How is the crediting rate determined?

How often can the crediting rate change?

What is the current general account return of the carrier?

Does this policy contain a no-lapse guarantee?
If so, how long does it last?

What happens to the no-lapse guarantee in the event of a missed premium?

Can missed premiums be made up to reinstate the no-lapse provision?

How can policy expenses change and how would you be notified?

How can mortality costs change and how would you be notified?

What riders are illustrated?

What is the loan rate of this policy?
Is it variable or fixed?

How is the loan rate determined?

How long do surrender charges last?

Did you follow the Life Insurance Underwriting Process Guideline Checklist?

Have you been provided with a financial profile on the carrier (such as ALIRT or VitalSigns)?

Is there an "early cash value" (ECV) rider available?

If ECV is available, have you compared it to a non-ECV contract?

Were you provided a final illustration that *exactly* matches the policy that was issued?

Have you verified that ownership and beneficiary designations are correct?

Has your agent committed to providing you an in-force ledger at least every two years?

Are there carrier incentives tied to the sale of this policy?

Indexed Universal Life Policy Purchase Checklist

Indexed universal life insurance is a complicated product with segment rate, expense, and mortality risk. The biggest mistakes we see with indexed policies pertain to crediting rates: policies illustrated at rates that cannot be substantiated. Be sure to request the rationale used to determine the policy-crediting rate illustrated. As with universal life insurance, the most common problems we see are policies not performing as projected, which generally means that the policy will lapse prior to the insured's death.

The answers to the questions on this checklist will help determine whether an indexed universal life policy will perform as projected and whether it will meet your needs.

CARRIER / POLICY NAME:
Carrier Rating AM Best:
Carrier Rating Comdex:
Carrier Rating ALIRT:
Is the carrier on any rating company's watch list?
Is there any public information on the carrier that could affect future ratings?
What is the crediting rate illustrated?
What is the minimum interest rate guarantee?

Did you receive an illustration at 1
percent below current crediting rate?

How are indexed crediting rates
determined?

How often are indexed crediting rates
determined?

How was the illustrated rate
determined?

Does this policy contain a no-lapse guarantee? If so, how long does it last?

What happens to the no-lapse guarantee in the event of a missed premium?

Can missed premiums be made up to
reinstate the no-lapse provision?

How can policy expenses change and
how would you be notified?

How can mortality costs change and
how would you be notified?

What riders are illustrated?

What is the loan rate of policy?
Is it variable or fixed?

How is the loan rate determined?

How long do surrender charges last?

Did you follow the Life Insurance
Underwriting Process Guideline Checklist?

Have you been provided with a
financial profile on the carrier
(such as ALIRT or VitalSigns)?

Is there an "early cash value" (ECV)
rider available?

If ECV is available, have you compared
it to a non-ECV contract?

Were you provided a final illustration that
exactly matches the policy that was issued?

Have you verified that ownership and
beneficiary designations are correct?

Has your agent committed to providing
you an in-force ledger at least every two
years?

Are there carrier incentives tied to the
sale of this policy?

Variable Life Policy Purchase Checklist

Variable life insurance is a complicated product subject to investment, expense, and mortality risk. We often see policies illustrated at rates that cannot be substantiated. Request the rationale used to determine the policy-crediting rate illustrated. The most common problems we see are policies not performing as projected, which generally means that the policy will lapse prior to the insured's death. Variable policies are often not allocated according to a diversified investment strategy, but are instead consistently invested in overly expensive funds. That combination can lead to poor policy performance, which can cause the policy to fail to meet the owner's objectives.

The answers to the questions in this checklist will help you determine whether a variable policy will perform as projected and whether it will meet your needs.

CARRIER / POLICY NAME:
Carrier Rating AM Best:
Carrier Rating Comdex:
Carrier Rating ALIRT:
Is the carrier on any rating company's watch list?
Is there any public information on the carrier that could affect future ratings?

What is the crediting rate illustrated?

What is the minimum interest guarantee?

Did you receive an illustration at 2 percent below current dividend-crediting rate?

Have you been provided a prospectus? (You must have this!)

What subaccounts are being recommended?

Are projected returns based on subaccount historical performance?

Have the expenses of the subaccounts been analyzed to pick efficient fund allocations?

Does this policy contain a no-lapse guarantee? If so, how long does it last?

What happens to the no-lapse guarantee in the event of a missed premium?

Can missed premiums be made up to reinstate the no-lapse provision?

How can policy expenses change and how would you be notified?

How can mortality costs change and how would you be notified?

What riders are illustrated?

What is the loan rate of policy?

Is it variable or fixed?

How is the loan rate determined?

How long do surrender charges last?

Did you follow the Life Insurance Underwriting Process Guideline Checklist?

Have you been provided with a financial profile on the carrier (such as ALIRT or VitalSigns)?

Is there an "early cash value" (ECV) rider available?

If ECV is available, have you compared it to a non-ECV contract?

Were you provided a final illustration that *exactly* matches the policy that was issued?

Have you verified that ownership and beneficiary designations are correct?

Has your agent committed to providing an in-force ledger at least every two years?

Are there carrier incentives tied to the sale of this policy?

Joint "Last To Die" Policies

Second-to-die policies are commonly purchased by affluent clients and can be a very effective tool for paying estate taxes if structured properly. These policies come in many forms, and therefore it is important to determine which type of policy you are considering. Once you have determined which type of policy would work best for you, apply the appropriate checklist to that purchase. You must also ask if there are any changes in how the policy premium and costs work after the death of the first insured.

Fraud

We would like to assume that anyone you choose to deal with is acting in your best interests, but unfortunately this isn't always the case. We believe that these checklists can be used as a tool to prevent fraudulent activity, though we don't advertise them as such.

It is important that we recognize that fraud exists and to reiterate that while this book cannot protect you from fraudulent agents, these questions can help to clarify their acumen regarding

**Steps to Achieving
Our Definition of Success**

__X__ **Obstacles**
__X__ **Advisor**
__X__ **Policy**
_____ **Underwriting**
_____ **Maintenance**

this industry. At the very least, these checklists can help you detect if someone is attempting to misrepresent or twist product offerings.

TREAD LIGHTLY

CHAPTER 4

STEP THREE:

UNDERWRITING PROCESS GUIDE

Now that you understand some of the key issues you face in finding an advisor and purchasing a policy, you'll want to secure that policy at the best possible price.

A consumer should never submit an application before the advisor and underwriting team have full knowledge of the client's entire underwriting file; this includes the insured's complete medical history (medications taken, past and current medical conditions, and family history). In addition, it is important to know the client's travel history, driving record, avocations, citizenship, financial status, and purpose of insurance. Only then can an advisor negotiate with prospective carriers for the best product and rates possible within the marketplace.

This is why a proprietary underwriting process is so important. The problem of submitting an application prior to having a completed profile is that it gives leverage and control to the carrier. Presenting a full and comprehensive file to the carrier with a professional underwriting opinion will help you get the pricing you deserve. It also makes the carrier-underwriter's job easier and helps the underwriter be more efficient.

Be sure to inquire about a firm's placement rate with carriers. The higher the placement rate, the more profitable business is to the carrier. Oftentimes carriers will be more receptive to an advisor's recommendation when his or her agency has a high placement rate.

It has been said before in this book, but it bears repeating: any time you are dealing with prospective advisors in the life insurance industry, have them explain their underwriting department, process, and support staff. It is important to understand how their firm operates before you make a commitment to any agency.

The key to finding an effective underwriting advocate is to locate a firm with both medical and multicarrier underwriting knowledge. It is preferable that your advisory firm has someone on its team with extensive medical knowledge, preferably an MD, so that the advisor and the underwriting department can assist you in building your file in the most honest and favorable light possible.

The underwriting process should all be completed and evaluated before submitting anything to *any* carrier. Completing this process leads to higher placement rates, which results in more profitable business with the carriers. More profitable business for the carriers creates room for underwriting to be more aggressive when needed, and that entire dynamic usually leads to better offers for clients.

Underwriting Checklist

Once you have made the decision to purchase life insurance, you must follow a specific process to generate the best possible outcome and results. We recommend the following:

1. _____ Sign a generic multicarrier HIPAA form giving your agent and agency the ability to negotiate with numerous insurance carriers.

   Additionally, sign a laboratory release form to allow the agency to request lab results for review (most carriers won't comply until a formal application has been submitted).

2. _____ Complete an informal application disclosing all relevant information to your advisor so that a complete profile can be developed for informal application submissions.

3. _____ Provide a complete listing of *all* medical providers seen over the past ten years.

4. _____ Provide a complete list of all medications taken over the past five years, including dosage amounts.

5. _____ Schedule your insurance exam (the agency will do this for you).

6. _____ Read and follow the Medical Exam Guide prior to an insurance exam (included in the following pages and on *www.TreadLightlyGuide.com*).

7. _____ If you have any medical or nonmedical conditions, make sure your agent is negotiating with a carrier(s) that specifically targets those conditions.

8. _____ Deal only with an agent who has a third-party or in-house MD and/or underwriting specialist available to negotiate with carriers on your behalf. Request this individual's credentials so you may evaluate his or her experience.

9. _____ Require a list of carriers being considered and the reason for final selection of the insurance company your advisor recommends.

10. _____ Review illustrations comparing final offers to determine whether the selected carrier meets your needs.

11. _____ Submit a formal application to obtain issued policy.

Once a formal application has been submitted, underwriting can take anywhere from one to approximately eight weeks. Occasionally the underwriter may come back and ask for additional information or forms. The more information collected and submitted at the time of formal submission, the faster the underwriting process.

After you have completed your exam and the formal application is submitted, the carrier will come back with an offer. Make sure you talk with your agent and understand your offer.

Medical Exam Guide

As part of your application for life insurance, a medical exam will be required. Either a paramedical company will complete this report or a medical doctor will be contracted by the insurance carrier. The examiner will schedule the appointment at a time and place that is convenient for you. This includes your home, office, or the examiner's office; you should make the decision that best fits your schedule.

Since your life insurance rates will be directly affected by the findings on the exam, it is important to follow the guidelines below to generate the best results possible:

- Drink plenty of water the day before the exam.

- Try to get a good night's sleep the night before.

- Limit high-salt, high-fat, and high-cholesterol foods for twenty-four hours before the exam.

- Have a list of your current and past physicians' names, addresses, dates of visits, and the medications they have prescribed you for at least the past five years.

- Schedule your exam as early in the morning as is practical.

- Void early in the morning prior to the examination. Afterward, drink a glass of water one hour before the appointment to facilitate obtaining a urine specimen.

- Avoid drinking coffee, tea, or any caffeinated beverages before your exam. The caffeine can temporarily raise your blood pressure and increase your pulse.

- Refrain from strenuous exercise for forty-eight hours before your exam. Heavy exercise can temporarily elevate liver test results and cause protein in your urine sample.

- Avoid drinking alcohol forty-eight hours before the exam. Alcohol can negatively influence blood pressure, pulse, and liver tests.

- Try to not use any tobacco or nicotine products for at least an hour before your exam. These products can temporarily raise your blood pressure and pulse. If you use noncigarette tobacco periodically and are applying for nontobacco rates, avoid tobacco usage at least seven days prior to the exam.

- A blood sample taken while fasting better optimizes lipid, liver, and sugar tests. Each company has different requirements, but an overnight fast with the exam done early in the morning is preferred.

- Don't forget your photo ID. This is required by the examiner to verify your identity.

- Wear a short-sleeved shirt or a shirt with sleeves that can be easily rolled up.

- If you need a large blood pressure cuff, let the examiner know when you are scheduling your exam.

- If you weigh more than three hundred pounds, please let the examiner know when you are scheduling your exam.

- Avoid taking any over-the-counter medications and vitamins for twenty-four hours before the exam. Advil and nasal decongestants, for example, can elevate liver tests, and many weight-lifting supplements affect kidney tests.

- If you are feeling sick, don't be afraid to cancel your appointment. Having the best possible exam will help you get the best possible rating.

These tests are performed at no extra cost to you and are paid for by the insurance company, but you have a right to know the results. Some insurance companies have started automatically mailing lab results to the client's home, but we encourage you to request that the carrier send you your exam results. It is preferable to obtain the entire exam including labs and have your advisor's underwriting department review them before submission of a formal application.

Steps to Achieving Our Definition of Success

- **X** **Obstacles**
- **X** **Advisor**
- **X** **Policy**
- **X** **Underwriting**
- ____ **Maintenance**

Visit www.TreadLightlyGuide.com/Medical for a request form that you can print out to obtain your lab results.

CHAPTER 5

STEP FOUR:
HOW TO PROPERLY MAINTAIN
YOUR POLICY

It is crucial that you understand that maintaining a life insurance policy doesn't stop at the time of purchase.

Just like your overall financial strategy, your life insurance philosophy must be dynamic; as your goals change, so should your coverage.

The Eight Biggest Risks to Policy Maintenance

As technology, health-care improvements, and access to information changes, life insurance products evolve and improve. More often than not, this results in greater values and less expensive offerings with a higher overall quality.

The policies available today are far better products than in previous generations and will continue to improve. If you currently own an insurance policy or represent the interests of an insurance policy owner, we have listed some key reasons why this insurance should be reviewed periodically (we recommend a review every two years, at minimum.)

Keep in mind that carriers are large corporations that deal with thousands of employees and an even larger number of clients. Mistakes happen, and you can't always rely on the carrier to act in your best interest.

Ownership and Beneficiary Designations

We often find that the ownership and beneficiary designations of an in-force policy do not match the client's objectives. Typically, clients' needs for life insurance will change throughout their financial lives. As clients' finances evolve, so does their need for better and more complex options. As the purpose of insurance changes from simply providing for a spouse or paying off debts, to estate settlement purposes and more, these ownership and beneficiary designations have to reflect the client's updated needs.

Variable Life Insurance

Given the market returns in the past, many of these policies will not have the ability to last until life expectancy, and they will either require substantially more premium or lapse. The primary risk with variable insurance is investment risk. As negative market returns occur while mortality expenses increase, variable policies have very little chance of recovering without a substantial infusion of additional premiums. Make sure you review the investment allocation of the subaccounts on every policy review, paying particular attention to fund expenses and diversification.

Whole Life, Universal Life, And Indexed Life

The same threats that apply to existing variable insurance also apply to existing whole, universal, and indexed life policies. In these cases, interest rates over the past twenty-five years have decreased so drastically that many in-force contracts are not performing at a level even close to what was initially projected, and many will lapse.

Declining Mortality Costs

Modern medicine has enabled Americans to live considerably longer than previous generations. This trend is reflected in the mortality tables used by the life insurance industry today and, in turn, affects how much these contracts cost.

A mortality table is a set of information used by actuaries to determine the probability of a person's age at death. These tables are used as a guide to assess mortality risk and determine an expected lifespan of any given client.

It normally takes at least three to four years for these tables to be built into the price of new policies. Product development is very slow in this industry. Current mortality tables are based on information from 2001; therefore, any policy issued between 2005 and 2006 (or before) is likely based on substantially higher mortality costs. Before the 2001 table update, insurance carriers were using formulas based on the previous structure, which was created in 1980. If you look at 1980 mortality tables versus the 2001 set, the difference is significant. Mortality tables will change and likely improve over the course of your life insurance ownership, so be aware when these changes occur so you can determine whether the new mortality tables present you with an opportunity to improve your portfolio.

General Expense and Commission Reductions

Like most industries, costs continue to follow downward pressure, providing a better product for the consumer. It costs less to buy life insurance today than ever before.

It is also valuable to note that as consumers and consumer advocates have grown to require more transparency from carriers, various carrier costs and charges have changed. This has also driven down general policy expenses, and the result is a better competitive market.

An agent today also makes less commission in renewals than in previous decades. This allows the carrier to sell a more competitive policy and pass the savings on to the consumer. Unfortunately, it also creates an environment where consumers aren't getting the guidance they deserve because there is less agent incentive to service the insurance.

Better Rate Classes Now Exist for the Consumer

Rate class is defined as the underwriting class (and ultimately determined by the carrier) and reflects the price at which the insured can purchase a policy.

Better rate classes that were not available until recently now exist for the consumer. Ratings such as *preferred*, *super preferred*, *standard plus*, and *preferred tobacco* were not available in the past, and this specialization is crucial in making new policies more competitive; rate classes will improve as medicine and research continues to advance.

Carriers have and will become more aggressive in underwriting certain conditions that had previously resulted in declines, postpones, or ratings requiring extra premium. For all the above reasons and more, we recommend a complete policy review at least every two years.

As your health condition changes over time, so might the underwriting of an existing policy. If the carrier becomes more aggressive on a health condition or your health improves, inquire about your existing policies as to whether an in-force rate class reduction is available on that contract. If so, your policy could become less expensive and might perform much better than what was projected based on the original rate class issue.

Policy Riders Have Significantly Improved

Policy riders are additional benefits added to policies at a cost to help policyholders better accomplish their goals. Features such as long-term care, continuation after age one hundred, overloan protection, and no-lapse guarantees provide clients with far superior products that didn't exist at their current levels of sophistication and value when many consumers purchased their existing policies.

Legislation and Tax Law Changes

Changes in legislation and tax law can affect the efficacy of an in-force policy, as they can cause existing policies to fail to accomplish their intended strategies. The policy review process must consider these changes with regard to their impact on your portfolio.

Remember, the ultimate goal is to *end up with the right policy at the appropriate price, with the right carrier for your needs, and a responsible, long-term maintenance strategy so that the policy pays off at the insured's death.* This is what we ultimately consider a "good deal" when buying insurance.

How to Maintain Your Policy

Do you know for certain that your policy is adequately funded and meeting your objectives to achieve our definition of success? To ensure that your life insurance is properly funded and is actively meeting your financial goals, we have developed the following guidelines to maintain your insurance portfolio.

Retain the Final Sales Illustration

Retain the final illustration that was presented during the purchase or delivery of your policy. It should be an exact match to the policy declaration page. Make sure all riders listed are part of that illustration. If you do not have original final illustration of your purchase, request it from the agent and/or carrier. The carrier likely based the issuance of your policy on that final illustration.

Update Ratings

Carriers' financial status changes frequently, so it is important to assess the ongoing financial quality of your carrier at least every two years. Make sure that assessment is based on the actual carrier that issued your policy and is not based solely on the parent company.

In-force Ledgers Request Guide

Request an in-force ledger from the existing insurance company at least every two years. What you ask for depends on the policy purchased. The variations are:

Term Policy Ledger Request

Request an in-force ledger projecting future premiums as well as the terms of the conversion option.

Whole Life Policy Ledger Request

Request an in-force ledger at least every two years based on the current dividend-crediting rate and 1 percent below the current dividend-crediting rate. Inquire as to what their current dividend-crediting rate is based on and when it could be expected to change.

Request a written explanation regarding their dividend-crediting strategy. Also request a disclosure on what the insurance company's current return is on its general account. Compare in-force illustrations to original projections. Consider the current crediting rate as compared to general account return and further request the carrier's crediting philosophy.

If the current crediting rate is above the general account return, ask the carrier how that is achieved.

Universal Life Policy Ledger Request

Request an in-force ledger every two years based on the current crediting rate and 1 percent below. You should also request a disclosure on what the insurance company's current return is on its general account.

Compare the in-force ledger to its original projection. If the policy is projected to lapse before age one hundred (earlier or later, if you choose), ask what premium increase would be necessary to keep the policy in-force until that time. Ask if there has been a mortality cost or expense change in the past year and if so, what the amount was. If there is a no-lapse provision in the policy, inquire if it is current or how much would need to be paid to bring it current.

If the current crediting rate is above the general account return, ask the carrier how that is achieved.

Variable Life Policy Ledger Request

Request an in-force ledger at least every two years based on an assumed rate of return that you expect the subaccounts to produce. Ask for a second illustration at 2 percent below that rate.

Compare in-force ledgers to original projections. If the policy is projected to lapse prior to age one hundred (earlier or later, if you choose), ask what premium increase is necessary to keep the policy in-force until that time. Ask for a listing of how the cash values are invested and in which subaccounts. Consider that allocation and whether it is currently applicable.

Ask for a list of all subaccounts available along with a fund expense disclosure and historical returns. Consider reallocating funds periodically due to current circumstances. Monitor the subaccount allocations regularly.

Ask if there has been a mortality cost or expense change in the past year and if so, what the amount was.

Indexed Universal Life Ledger Request

Request an in-force ledger at least every two years based on the current crediting rate and 1 percent below. Inquire as to their general account current return. Compare the in-force ledger to its original projection. If the policy is projected to lapse before age one hundred (earlier or later, if you choose), ask what premium increase would be necessary to keep the policy in-force until that time.

Request a summary of which indexed funds the cash value is allocated toward. Request a list of other available indexed funds along with historical returns and consider the allocation of those funds periodically due to current circumstances.

Ask if there has been a mortality cost or expense change in the past year and if so, what was the amount. If there is a no-lapse provision in the policy, inquire if it is current or how much would need to be paid to bring it current.

Biannual Requests

At least every two years, no matter what type of insurance you own, you should request from the carrier:

- Owner of the policy
- Beneficiary of the policy
- Address of record of owner

The agent that sold you the policy should be willing to provide this information to you every two years with no effort on your part. If you do not get this commitment from the agent, consider changing the agent of record on the policy to someone that will commit to providing this information on your behalf for the duration of your policy ownership.

Visit *www.TreadLightlyGuide.com/inforce* for copies of these checklists and download whichever documents pertain to the policy you own. We have also provided sample in-force ledger request letters to make your request for this information easier to carry out.

Irrevocable Life Insurance Trust Checklist

Most affluent people buy life insurance within a vehicle called an Irrevocable Life Insurance Trust (ILIT). Typically the insured(s) is the *grantor* and the children are the *beneficiaries* of the trust. The selection of the trustee is a very big decision and one of the most important steps in the establishment of the trust, as that person or entity has the fiduciary responsibility to follow certain steps so that the trust is in compliance with ILIT rules.

The reasons for selecting an ILIT are many, but it is only effective if the ILIT is structured and managed properly. When this is the case, an ILIT becomes a wonderful and effective tax-leverage strategy. The trustee within an ILIT should monitor the following procedures:

1. _____ The trustee should apply for and own the policy by following a credible application and underwriting process. The grantor should never sign as owner or anything other than the insured prior to the establishment of the trust.

2. _____ Premiums should be contributed by the grantor to the trust utilizing an annual gifting strategy. Once premiums are received by the trust, the trustee then notifies the beneficiaries of the trust that a gift has been made on behalf of the beneficiaries. The beneficiaries are then given a limited period of time to withdraw their portion of that gift, or the right to make a withdrawal lapses. The trustee then pays the premium to the carrier.

3. _____ All premiums should be paid by the trustee to the carrier from the trust checking account.

4. _____ The grantor should retain proof of the gifts contributed to the trust. The trustee should retain a copy of referenced notices above along with proof that those notices were sent.

5. _____ The trustee should request an in-force ledger at least every two years to determine whether the policy still meets trust objectives; then they should follow our process (or one that is similar) for policy review. The trustee should retain all materials pertaining to these reviews to provide proof of fiduciary due diligence.

If the above procedures are followed, the desired tax leverage (gift, estate, and income tax) should be attained.

Steps to Achieving
Our Definition of Success

X **Obstacles**
X **Advisor**
X **Policy**
X **Underwriting**
X **Maintenance**

The desired tax leverage is based on the death proceeds. These proceeds should be payable to the trust without any income or gift taxation and should be excluded from the decedent's estate for estate tax purposes.

CHAPTER 6

THE CONVERSATION
THAT NEVER ENDS

As I've stated several times, my ultimate goal is to educate as many people as I can about how to be informed life insurance consumers so they can make the best insurance maintenance and purchasing decisions possible.

I hope you use the materials in this book and the tools on our website, and that this publication ultimately benefits you in the purchase or maintenance of your life insurance portfolio. We live in a time where information is more readily available than ever before. This industry has been slow to change, and, unfortunately, there will always be agents who do not want to see tools like these in the hands of the consumer.

However, anyone who applies these principles to their buying or maintenance processes will make their own agents work harder, and in turn, make their agents that much more knowledgeable about the industry. The harder we work to understand what we are selling, the more confident we can be that our clients are buying the appropriate products that will last until their deaths.

In this case, however strange it may sound, reaching the finish line means that when you die, your insurance policy has paid off at your death. Remember our definition of success, and let it be an anchor throughout the entirety of your life insurance ownership.

My goal was to provide a short but sweet high-level overview of the information you will need to ensure that the policies in question are being properly handled and maintained by honest, trustworthy advisors. If every advisor follows a process similar to those outlined in *Tread Lightly*, we can begin to ensure that all clients achieve their objectives.

But we're not done yet. This industry is changing rapidly, and our website, *www.TreadLightlyGuide.com*, will be used as a continually evolving tool to keep you educated and answer your industry-specific questions. The worst of our industry is receding now that we live in a new age of accountability and transparency. We now have the tools to fix what is broken and reinforce a foundation of ethics, protection, and advocacy.

Hopefully the information contained here was enough to put you in a direction of forward momentum. If it wasn't, I'd love to know what other information you would like to see covered in the future. In this age of social media and instant communication, we want to continue to connect, assess, identify, and collaborate. Don't hesitate to visit *www.TreadLightlyGuide.com* with any questions, and we'll do our best to help you any way we can.

Let's keep the conversation going.

APPENDIX

Tracking the Financial Health of Your Insurance Carriers

Everything in this book talks about analyzing, planning for, and devising the best life insurance strategy for the customer. But the best-laid life insurance plans are for naught if the contract on which they are based does not ultimately perform.

An insurance policy is a legal contract between the insured and a specific insurance company listed on the policy's declaration page. This contract lays out what it covers in very precise language, and for how much and under what circumstances the insurer is obliged to fulfill its promise. With a life insurance policy, for example, an insurer agrees to pay a stipulated amount of money to a specified beneficiary upon the death of the insured.

But what if, at the insured's time of death, the insurer is under financial duress and does not have the funds to make good on its promise? Sadly, in this case the beneficiary has no legal recourse except to wait for partial or (hopefully) full payment over time through a legal receivership or liquidation process and/or through a state-guaranteed fund mechanism. State fund guarantees are generally limited, so if one is buying large amounts of insurance, these agencies tend to be minimally helpful.

Therefore, when acquiring a life insurance policy, the insured should pay close attention to the financial well-being of the company issuing the policy. How is this best accomplished?

There are a number of common options to consider when reviewing a company's financial strength:

- Public rating agencies
- Comdex Scores
- ALIRT Analyses
- Performing your own financial review

We cover each of these briefly below.

Public Rating Agencies

Public rating agencies are companies that specialize in analyzing the financial position of insurance companies and providing opinions on their current ability to pay claims. These opinions are expressed in the form of a letter rating.

The four big public ratings agencies are A.M. Best Company, Fitch Ratings, Moody's Investor Services, and Standard & Poor's, each of which is designated a Nationally Recognized Statistical Rating Organization (NRSRO) by the US government. Each company's insurance letter ratings can be accessed for free on each rater's website, though you'll need to pay an additional amount for a more in-depth analysis of that letter rating.

Several of the "big four" rating agencies use different rating and letter scales, which can be confusing at first (see below). Each letter rating is also assigned a qualitative descriptor, also detailed below. It is important to note that the same letter rating from two different insurers can mean different things based on the related descriptor. Generally, however, the higher the letter rating, the stronger the perceived claims-paying ability of that company.

A fifth rating agency, which is not an NRSRO, is Weiss Ratings. Weiss tracks the financial strength of life insurance companies on a quarterly basis and sells one-page reports to consumers and producers that summarize the important factors behind an insurer's rating.

Rating Scales and Definitions

Moody's Description	S&P Description	Fitch Description	A.M. Best Description	Weiss Description
Aaa – Exceptional Aa – Excellent A – Good Baaa – Adequate	AAA – Exceptional Strong AA – Very Strong A – Strong BBB – Good	AAA – Exceptional Strong AA – Very Strong A – Strong BBB – Good	A++, A+ – Superior A, A- – Excellent B++, B+ – Good	A – Excellent B – Good
Ba – Questionable B – Poor Caa – Very Poor Ca – Extremely Poor C – Lowest	BB – Marginal B – Weak CCC – Very Weak CC – Extremely Weak R – Regulatory Supervision	BB – Moderately Weak B – Weak CCC, CC, C – Very Weak DDD, DD, D – Distressed	B, B- – Fair C++, C+ – Marginal C, C- – Weak D – Poor E – Regulatory Supervision	C – Fair D – Weak E – Very Weak + = upper 1/3 of grade range - = lower 1/3 of grade range

Comdex Scores

Given the complexity of the different rating agencies' scales, the Comdex Score was developed to help simplify the expression of insurer financial strength. The Comdex Score is not a rating in itself, but rather a composite of all the ratings a company has received from the big four rating agencies.

Essentially, the Comdex is derived by ranking insurance company ratings from each agency from high to low, them separating them into deciles. The relative position of each insurer in this ranking structure determines its Comdex Score, which can range from 0 to 100. The higher the score, the higher the ratings are for an insurer relative to its peers, and thus, the higher perceived financial strength of that carrier.

Comdex Scores can be accessed through the VitalSigns service, which is subscription based. The VitalSigns Suite includes additional financial information about insurance companies, including five-year trends of selected financial metrics, which can be compared between carriers as well as to an industry composite. This information is updated on an annual basis.

ALIRT Analyses

An ALIRT Analysis is a two-page document that provides a holistic view of an insurance company's financial condition. The first page consists of financial metrics that provide approximately fifty inputs across four tiers of risk, including the four major agency ratings. This information is included on a time-trended basis and is compared to an industry composite.

The second page is a scorecard that converts each of the financial metrics into scores, resulting in a total ALIRT Score (with a range of 0 to 100). The higher the score, the stronger the relative financial position of that insurer. These analyses are updated on a quarterly basis.

Unlike rating agencies and Comdex, ALIRT integrates its analyses into a comprehensive service that provides its clients with access to its analysts for point-of-sale and other support. For this reason, ALIRT can be viewed as an advisor's outsourced due diligence staff.

Performing Your Own Financial Review

A final option is to perform your own analysis of carrier financial strength. In an ideal world, this might be considered the best option, though lack of time, expertise, and desire to undertake this level of work often make this an unrealistic task for a financial advisor.

Despite all this, all of the elements necessary for an independent financial review are available for no or little cost.

Insurers are required to file quarterly statutory financial filings with their respective insurance departments, which are available either directly from these state departments or, increasingly, from insurers' own websites. VitalSigns is owned by publicly traded Ibex Inc., and these analyses are produced by privately held ALIRT Insurance Research LLC.

Another option is to access state financial filings through the National Association of Insurance Commissioners (NAIC) website. A third option is to buy the quarterly statutory and GAAP financial filings from a number of data providers, including SNL and the AM Best Company.

Additionally, the publicly traded parents of many insurance companies are required to file quarterly GAAP financial statements, though these filings provide a financial overview of the entire holding company and not the insurer's financials specifically. As previously mentioned, the public ratings (but not Comdex or ALIRT Scores) are also available free of charge.

Once this data is gathered, ideally on a several-year-trend basis, you must have a basic understanding of an insurer's balance sheet, income statement, and cash flow page in order to draw educated conclusions about the relative financial condition of a prospective insurer.

Again, while this is perhaps an ideal option, practically speaking, independent examinations of insurers are often not an option for insurance agents.

Conclusions

When determining the best course of action, it is important to keep several things in mind:

1. **Since an insurance policy is a legal contract between the insured and a specific insurance entity, it is very important to focus on the financial strength of that particular insurer and not the insurer's parent.** Remember, if an insurance company gets into financial trouble, its parent holding company is under no legal obligation to bail it out (unless there is a specific agreement in place to that end, and even these are not foolproof).

   Unfortunately, the public rating agency methodology —and by extension, Comdex—places great emphasis on the implicit financial support of the parent agency. The problem here is that ratings can change overnight, at times dramatically, if the specific insurer is no longer essential to the parent holding company. As you can see in the below graphic, there has been widespread change in insurance company ownership over just the past fifteen years, with the inevitable whipsawing of ratings.

   The best bet is to always focus on the financials of the actual company to which the insured has legal exposure first; again, look to the declaration page for this information. ALIRT Research and Weiss Ratings are your best bets in this regard.

Partial List of Ownership Changes Last Fifteen Years		Demutualizations in Period 1997–2001	
American General	Lincoln Benefit Life	AmerUs*	97
American Skandia	Liberty Life (Athene Life & Annuity)	American United/OneAmerica MHC	00
AmerUs/AVIVA Life & Annuity/Athene	Lincoln	Americas/UNIFI	97
Canada Life	National/Jefferson-Pilot Life	Canada Life*	99
Columbus Life	Metlife Investors USA	General American* MHC	97
Commonwealth Annuity & Life (Allmerica)	Presidential Life	Indianapolis Life*	01
Crown Life	Provident Mutual	John Hancock*	00
Equitable Life Assurance	Reliance Standard	Manufacturers Life	99
Equitrust Life	Reliastar Life	Metropolitan Life	00
Fidelity & Guaranty	Riversource (IDS)	Minnesota Life MHC	98
Forethought Life	Security Benefit	MONY Life*	98
General American	Shenandoah Life	National Life of VT MHC	98
Genworth Life & Annuity	SunAmerica	Ohio National MHC	98
Indianapolis Life	Sun Life of Canada (US) /Delaware Life	Pacific Life MHC	97
ING Life & Annuity (Aetna Life & Annuity)	Safeco Life/Symetra Life	Phoenix Life	01
Integrity Life	Transamerica	Principal Life	98
John Hancock / Manufacturers Life USA	Travelers - Citi - Metlife	Prudential	00
Lafayette Life	Union Central Life	Security Benefit* MHC	98
	Zurich/Kemper	Standard Ins. Co.	99
Courtesy of ALIRT Insurance Research		Sun Life*	00
		Western & Southern MHC	00
		Woodmen Accident & Life/Assurity MHC	99

2. **Financial due diligence must be ongoing.** We cannot stress this enough. None of the tracking options discussed above involves a crystal ball, which is to say that neither public ratings, nor an ALIRT Score, nor your own analysis will tell you what the financial position of a company will be three, five, ten, or twenty years down the road. Many unpredictable variables are constantly impinging upon the performance of an insurer: capital market movements, management changes, product changes, regulatory and legislative changes, and most importantly, potential changes in ownership.

Given these factors, the responsible approach after buying a policy is to track the financial performance of that company on a regular basis. This can be done by periodically checking ratings or ratings outlooks (rating agencies place various outlooks on their own ratings, including *positive*, *stable*, *negative*, *evolving*, etc.), tracking changes in Comdex or ALIRT Scores, or by refreshing your own financial analyses from time to time.

3. **Remember that the company you choose does not necessarily have to have the highest ratings or scores; it simply has to be an average solvent company that is able to meet its long-term obligations.** Highly rated companies such as the major US mutual life insurers can potentially charge more money and offer less product flexibility than other insurers, relying on the relative attractiveness of their financial strength to close sales. While there is nothing inherently wrong with contracting with these companies, the insurance buyer should weigh policy cost, product specs, quality of service, and financial dependability before making a final decision.

If the above is scrutinized in conjunction with the policyholder's risk tolerance, this will ultimately result in the best risk-reward decision that can be made, procuring you the best coverage at the most attractive price. To this end, there are no set rules. Some advisors look to public ratings in the A+ to AAA range or Comdex Scores of eighty and higher. ALIRT provides an ongoing statistical analysis showing a "normal" ALIRT Score range, which advisors often reference. It is interesting to note that ALIRT Scores, other ratings, and Comdex Scores can often say very different things about a company. Again, this has much to do with the fact that ALIRT looks at company-specific financials while ratings concentrate largely on the implicit strength of the parent.

In the end, with regard to these financial strength decisions, you have to determine your own risk tolerance.

ACKNOWLEDGMENTS

My Partners at TFP Brokerage

Kathy Donnelly, one of my partners, who works tirelessly to help our firm hold true to its promises and values. She is certainly one of the most knowledgeable and ethical professionals in our industry.

Mike Becher and *Austin Knowles*, for immediately recognizing the importance of this project to our firm and to our audience, and for providing me with the time and support to compile this book.

TFP Brokerage Staff

Meredith "Merdie" Walters, for putting up with me for over twenty years and supporting my efforts to establish a meaningful presence in this marketplace. Merdie has always approached our business with the most positive, supportive attitude that any operations manager could ever hope to apply to this industry.

Kelly Barba, for her enthusiasm for the project. Kelly's consistent willingness to do whatever is necessary to see that our clients are being treated fairly by the carriers is a unique quality in this industry.

Other Acknowledgments

To my friends and golf buddies for giving me a venue to enjoy our camaraderie while playing and laughing as hard as semi-normal, responsible adults can.

Eric Kiesshauer, for being not only a good friend, but for helping me clarify our transparent approach to being an advocate within the insurance business. Your guidance through countless situations has allowed me to identify our core values and create many of the processes we have in place today.

I'd also like to thank all previous coworkers, partners, management teams, carrier contacts, industry professionals, and other client advisors that we have worked with (such as CPAs, attorneys, and trust officers), who have always provided me with an opportunity to learn more about this business and the correct way to guide our clients.

*A very special thanks to Zac Basinger,
our director of marketing*

Zac has brought our company into the twenty-first century in a manner we simply could not have achieved without his knowledge and dedication.

I am especially thankful to Zac for his efforts related to this book. He spent countless hours after work and on weekends writing and editing, converting my thoughts and experience into words. While we continued to pile projects onto him, he demonstrated a commitment to excellence and enthusiasm for this project. He never once complained about the time and effort that he had to dedicate in order for us to accomplish our goal. That goal was to create a meaningful tool for anyone involved in a sizable insurance arrangement so that readers would have the tools necessary to accomplish their own objectives. We also wanted to back up this book with a website that would allow anyone interested to access those tools on an ongoing basis.

Congratulations, Zac—you did just that! You are a remarkable young man with an incredibly bright future in our firm and industry.

31290572R00067

Made in the USA
Charleston, SC
10 July 2014